Natas]

Teacher's Manual 1

Russian Step By Step for Children

Editor: Ellen Weaver, Trilla Watt

Cover: Natalia Illarionova

russianstepbystepforchildren.com

First Edition
Russian Step By Step for Children

Teacher's Manual 1

All rights reserved

Copyright © 2016 by Russian Step By Step

Revised and updated in 2018

No part of this book may be reproduced or transmitted in any form or by any means: electronic or mechanical, including photocopying, recording, or by any information storage and retrieval system, without written permission from the publisher.

ISBN-13   978-1537288215

ISBN-10:   1537288210

Printed in the United States of America

Contents

COURSE DESCRIPTION 5
General Recommendations for Teachers 7
Free Audio Component 7
LESSON PLANS 9
LESSON 1 10
Greetings 10
Reading Russian 11
Alphabet 11
Articles 17
Verb 'To Be' 18
Intonation 18
LESSON 2 19
Кто это? Что это? 19
Или 20
LESSON 3 23
Что это такое? 24
Personal Pronouns: я, он, она, они 24
Я Оля 25
Это/то 26
LESSON 4 29
Conjunctions 'а' and 'и' 29
Это мой чай 31

Names 32

LESSON 5 34

Ь, Ъ 35

Gender of the Nouns 36

Где? 37

LESSON 6 40

Personal Pronouns 42

Посчитаем! 0-10 44

TEST 1 45

Part 1 – Listening Comprehension and Spelling 46

Part 2 - Grammar and Vocabulary 49

GRAMMAR TABLES 54

Personal Pronouns 55

Numbers 55

DICTIONARIES 56

Russian-English Dictionary 57

English-Russian Dictionary 63

Course Description

Russian Step By Step for Children 1: is the first part of the *Russian Step By Step for Children* course and is geared towards private and group students. It consists of 6 lessons.

The goal of this book is to teach the students to read in Russian and to introduce basic grammar, such as pronunciation rules, gender of the nouns, personal pronouns, counting 0 – 10.

The grammar is introduced gradually, the vocabulary is expanded from lesson to lesson, and all the four language skills (speaking, grammar, comprehension and writing) are worked on step-by-step. The students practice speaking and comprehension, as well as learn to ask and answer questions.

Each level of the course *Russian Step By Step for Children* is intended for 12 hours of class work. The course includes a *Workbook*, *Audio* (Free Direct Download from the website), *Teacher's Manual, Power Point Slides, and a Games Supplement.*

Workbook contains phrases, dialogues, exercises with answer keys. The translation of the new vocabulary and grammar explanation in English are located at the back of the book in English.

Audio is an extremely important component of the *Russian Step By Step for Children* (you can download it form russianstepbystepchildren.com). Ensure that listening to the audio is part of homework assignments.

Teacher's Manual contains recommendations to teachers about how to work with the course, lesson plans, explanations of grammar in English, mirroring the grammar explanations from the *Workbook*, as well as all the texts and exercises (with answers) from the *Workbook*.

Power Point Slides are organized by lessons. The slides contain photos and illustrations that support each lesson's vocabulary and grammar points. This eliminates the need to spend time searching for visual aids supporting both the presentation of the material and its memorization.

Games are organized by lessons. They allow the students to practice the new grammar and vocabulary in a fun and interactive way.

General Recommendations for Teachers

1. We recommend that teachers familiarize themselves with the structure of the *Workbook*.

2. All the exercises from the *Workbook* can be done orally in class, and then given as homework to be done in writing. The repetition increases the rate with which the students learn the material.

3. Exercises with ![bee icon] should be done in writing.

4. Words in this level of the *Russian Step By Step for Children* course are given with stress marks, as it affects pronunciation.

5. This sign ![audio icon] indicates that there is a corresponding audio track. It is usually meant for homework. The more your students work with the audio at home, the better their progress in class will be.

6. The amount of grammar presented in the Grammar section of the Workbook is intentionally limited. It only covers the material presented in that lesson. We recommend to not add additional rules and exceptions. More will be introduced in the following lessons and steps.

7. The *Grammar and Translation* section at the end of the *Workbook* mirrors the six lessons from the Primary Course. There the students can find the translation of all new words and phrases, as well as grammar explanations in English.

8. At the end of the Teacher's Manual you will find a TEST that can be used during the last lesson to check the students' progress.

FREE Audio Component

By purchasing this book, you receive the **FREE audio** component right away!

We recommend teachers to download the audio component to their computer first. This way you will be ready to help your students with the audio download in case they have problems.

To access the complimentary **Direct Digital Audio Download** please:

- Go to RussianStepByStep.com

- Create your username and password (It can be really simple. The system might tell you that your password is too easy – ignore it and *go with your simple password*. The system will accept it anyway.)

- After registration you will receive an email to verify your email address. Press the verification link, and **you are ready to listen!**

- Choose the correct series through the top menu: Books > Children Series Age 7 – 16 > Step 1

- Download the audio Tracks to your computer

- If you have any questions, please email us at info@russianstepbystep.com

Lesson Plans

Lesson 1

Lesson Goal:

1) Greetings
2) Getting Aquatinted with the Alphabet
3) 13 Letters: **а, к, м, о, с, т, п, л, э, д, з, е, н**
4) Simple Positive Sentences
5) Questions and Positive & Negative Answers
6) Importance of Intonation
7) Unstressed **O** Rule
8) Simple Commands: Repeat, Listen, Please
9) Game: Name the Object

Greetings

1. 1. Greetings

There are several phrases that can be used as greetings in Russian: **здравствуйте, здравствуй, привет, добрый день, доброе утро**.... Often foreigners use the word **привет** as a greeting, because it's easy to pronounce. The word **привет** is a very informal greeting that can be used between close friends and relatives. Otherwise it sounds rude. For this reason, we will start with the most common Russian greeting that can be used in any situation: **здравствуйте**[1].

Здра̷ствуйте, (the letter **в** is not pronounced) = *Hello*

The word **здравствуйте** is quite difficult to pronounce – it has two combinations of three consonants together. First we will practice this word with each student, asking to pronounce it. Then we will divide this word into three syllables, recite it slowly and ask the students to repeat after you.

здра-вствуй-те

 2

---

[1] We will introduce other greetings later on.

Normally children don't have problems with learning this greeting. Don't worry, if your students don't pronounce the word **здравствуйте** correctly at the beginning. Ask them to practice the greeting at home by listening to the Track 2.

Start every lesson with this greeting and ask your students to use it as a reply.

Reading Russian

Even though the Cyrillic alphabet looks different from the Roman one, it is pretty easy to learn it. There are certain rules for reading, and if you know them, you will be able to read any word.

In the Russian alphabet, like in many others, letters have their names and corresponding sounds. For example, in English it is impossible for a foreigner to read the words: blood, poor, and floor correctly, unless the pronunciation is known. This does not happen in Russian.

In order to be able to read Russian, you must learn the sounds that the Russian letters make together with the rules.

Some of the letters are really easy, because they look very similar to the English ones, and make similar sounds: А, О, Т, Е, К, and С.

Some of them look different, but make similar sounds: Б, Г, Д, Ё, Ч, Ж, И.

Some of them look different and are pronounced differently: Щ, Ы, Ц.

And some of them look similar, but make different sounds: Р, Н, В, Х.

 Those are the tricky ones.

But, if you learn them slowly, step by step, they won't trick you later on. So, if you see a Russian word, you have a certain expectation of its pronunciation.

In the student's *Workbook*, Russian letters are not introduced in alphabetical order.

All Russian words in the *Workbook* are given with a stress mark. Knowing which vowel is stressed in the word is very important, because it affects the pronunciation.

Alphabet

1. 2. Read the alphabet with your students once, trying to understand how the letters are pronounced. Concentrate on the sounds (see transliteration column). In the beginning we will learn sounds and connect them with the printed letters.

We recommend introducing cursive after the students have learned printed letters.

Printed Letter	Script	Name in the Alphabet	Transcription	Similar Sound in English
А а	*Аа*	а	[a]	like **a** in f**a**ther
Б б	*Бб*	бэ	[b]	like **b** in **b**ook
В в	*Вв*	вэ	[v]	like **v** in **v**et
Г г	*Гг*	гэ	[g]	like **g** in **g**oose
Д д	*Дд*	дэ	[d]	like **d** in **d**rama
Е е	*Ее*	е	[ye]	like **ye** in **ye**t
Ё ё	*Ёё*	ё	[yo]	like **yo** in **yo**ga
Ж ж	*Жж*	жэ	[ʒ]	like **s** in trea**s**ure
З з	*Зз*	зэ	[z]	like **z** in **z**ebra
И и	*Ии*	и	[ee]	like **ee** in w**ee**k
Й й	*Йй*	и краткое	[y]	like **y** in bo**y**
К к	*Кк*	ка	[k]	like **k** in **k**itten
Л л	*Лл*	эль	[l]	like **l** in **l**amp
М м	*Мм*	эм	[m]	like **m** in **m**an
Н н	*Нн*	эн	[n]	like **n** in **n**ote
О о	*Оо*	о	[o]	like **o** in s**o**rt
П п	*Пп*	пэ	[p]	like **p** in **p**et
Р р	*Рр*	эр	[r]	like **r** in **r**ed
С с	*Сс*	эс	[s]	like **s** in **s**chool

Т т	*Тт*	тэ	[t]	like **t** in **t**oy
У у	*Уу*	у	[u]	like **oo** in m**oo**d
Ф ф	*Фф*	эф	[f]	like **f** in **f**ly
Х х	*Хх*	ха	[h]	like **h** in **h**at
Ц ц	*Цц*	цэ	[ts]	like **zz** in pi**zz**a
Ч ч	*Чч*	чэ	[ch]	like **ch** in **ch**air
Ш ш	*Шш*	ша	[sh]	like **sh** in **sh**awl
Щ щ	*Щщ*	ща	[shsh]	like **shsh** in English **sh**i**p**
ъ	.	твёрдый знак	-	*
ы	.	ы	[i]	like **i** in s**i**t
ь	.	мягкий знак	-	**
Э э	*Ээ*	э	[e]	like **e** in s**e**t
Ю ю	*Юю*	ю	[yu]	like **you** in **you**th
Я я	*Яя*	я	[ya]	like **ya** in **ya**rd

There are 33 letters in the Russian alphabet: 10 vowels, 21 consonants, and two letters which do not make any sounds by themselves. These are called the hard sign and the soft sign. We will learn about these two letters in Lesson 5.

1. 3. Introduce simple words from exercise 1.

Use slides or physical objects.

1. 4. As was mentioned earlier, reading in Russian is much easier than it might look, because Russian is a fairly phonetic language. In most cases each letter corresponds to one sound.

Introduce the following letters: **А а, К к, М м, О о, С с, Т т**.

Write the following words on the white board: **мама, папа, маска**.

Read them together with the students. Ask the students to write the words down.

1.5. Introducing 2 new letters: **П п, Л л**

$$\boxed{\text{А а, К к, М м, О о, С с, Т т, П п, Л л}}$$

Read the word **стол** together with your students. Write the word **лампа** on the white board. Ask the student to read it. Help the student to read this word, if he/she cannot do it. Teach the student how to read simple words: **мама, лампа** и т. д.

1.6. Do exercise 1 orally in class. Usually students cannot write fast at the beginning. Therefore, the teacher writes on the white board, and the students write in their notebooks. Students do all exercises in their *Workbooks* at home. It will give them good practice. Writing really helps in memorizing words.

Упражнение 1

Read the following words, then listen to the audio and repeat after the native speaker. After that, write the words down.

1. па́па_____   2. ма́ма _____

3. кот_____   4. стол_____

5. ла́мпа _____   6. сала́т _____

7. сок_____   8. ка́ска _____

1.7. Introducing the new letter **Э** and a simple positive statement

Э́то ма́ска.
This is a mask.

Э́то молоко́.
This is milk.

это = [эта]

Point out to the student the pronunciation of the letter **o** in the word **это**. The letter **o** is pronounced as **a**.

Rule: Unstressed O is pronounced as A.

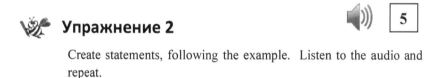

Упражнение 2

Create statements, following the example. Listen to the audio and repeat.

1. __Это мама.__　　2. __Это кот.__

3. __Это лампа.__　　4. __Это папа.__

5. __Это стол.__　　6. __Это салат.__

1.8. Introduce the letter **Д**. Teach how to ask simple questions and answer them with 'yes'.

- Это дом?
- Is this a house?

- Да, это дом.
- Yes, this is a house.

- Это мост?
- Is this a bridge?

- Да, это мост.
– Yes, this is a bridge.

 Упражнение 3

Create statements, following the example. Listen to the audio and repeat.

 1. _____ Это папа? Да, это папа. _____

2. _____ Это лампа? Да, это лампа. _____

3. _____ Это стол? Да, это стол. _____

4. _____ Это маска? Да, это маска. _____

 5. _____ Это салат? Да, это салат. _____

6. _____ Это молоко? Да, это молоко. _____

1.9. Repeat the greeting.

1.10. Introducing 3 new letters: **Е, З, Н**. Negative answers.

16

– Это молоко?
– *Is this milk?*

– Нет, это не молоко.
– *No, this is not milk.*

Это нóта.
This is a note.

– Это вода?
– *Is this water?*

– Нет, это не вода.
– *No, this is not water.*

Это знак «Стоп».
This is a Stop sign.

Articles

1. 11. There are no articles in Russian. Don't mention it, if the student does not ask about it. The student can read this rule in the *Workbook* in the Grammar section.

 Упражнение 4

Answer the questions, following the example.

1. Это сок? **Нет, это не сок. Это маска.**
2. Это молоко? **Нет, это не молоко. Это лампа.**
3. Это дом? **Нет, это не дом. Это стол.**
4. Это кот? **Нет, это не кот. Это дом.**
5. Это салат? **Нет, это не салат. Это мост.**
6. Это знак «Стоп»? **Нет, это не знак «Стоп». Это молоко.**
7. Это лампа? **Нет, это не лампа. Это нота.**

8.  Это маска?   Нет, это не маска. Это знак «Стоп».

Verb 'To Be'

1. 12. In most cases, the verb **быть**[2] (to be) is not used in the Present Tense. Again, don't mention that unless the student asks about it.

Intonation

1. 13. Questions are formed using a rising intonation. The word order is the same in affirmative and interrogative sentences.

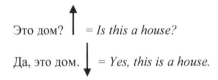

1. 14. Game for lesson 1 (You can purchase the downloadable from the website version.) It will make your lesson entertaining.

1. 15. Exercise 5 is the last exercise in the lesson. As was mentioned in the introduction, the last exercise in each lesson is aimed at comprehension. You will read the sentences aloud, while your students try to write them down. This will show your students how much they have actually learned. It may encourage them to spend more time on their homework.

The key to this exercise is not included in the *Workbook*. Therefore, this exercise is a small test for the students. The teacher can use it at the beginning of the next lesson to make sure the students are ready to move on.

Упражнение 5 - тест

1. Это стол. 2. Это папа. Это мама.   3. Это маска? Нет, это не маска. 4. Это знак «Стоп». 5. Это салат? Нет, это не салат. 6. Это нота? Нет, это не нота. 7. Это молоко? Да, это молоко. 8. Это кот? Да, это кот. 9. Это не мост. Это лампа.

---

[2] **есть** – the only form of the verb **быть** in the Present Tense

Lesson 2

Lesson Goal:

1) Three Letters: **Б, И, Ч**
2) General Questions: **Кто это? Что это?**
3) Questions with the Conjunction **или**
4) Letter **ф**
5) Game: Sort the Words

2. 1. Revision: What do we remember from the previous lesson? You can use the sentences from the homework.

2. 2. Three new letters: **Б, И, Ч**

New words: **чемпион, собака, диск**.

Кто это? Что это?

Это чемпион.	– Это кот?	– Это маска?
This is a champion.	– *Is this a cat?*	– *Is this a mask?*
	– Нет, это не кот.	– Нет, это не маска.
	– *No, this is not a cat.*	– *No, this is not a mask.*
	– Кто это?	– Что это?
	– *Who is this?*	– *What is this?*
	– Это собака.	– Это диск.
	– *This is a dog.*	*This is a* disk.

2.3. Teaching general questions: **Кто это? Что это?** Point out to your students the pronunciation of the letter **ч** in the word **что**.

Упражнение 6

Create a question for each statement, as in the example.

1. Это мама. __**Кто это?**__
2. Это нота. __**Что это?**__
3. Это папа. __**Кто это?**__
4. Это знак «Стоп». __**Что это?**__
5. Это салат. __**Что это?**__
6. Это пилот. __**Кто это?**__
7. Это молоко. __**Что это?**__
8. Это Анна. __**Кто это?**__
9. Это каска. __**Что это?**__

2. 4. Questions with the conjunction **или** (or)

Или

   9

– Это Том или Линда? — – Это пчела или собака?
– *Is this Tom or Linda?* — – *Is this a bee or a dog?*

– Это Линда. — – Это пчела.
– *This is Linda.* — – *This is a bee.*

2. 5. General questions: **Что это? Кто это?**

 Упражнение 7   10

Answer 'or' questions, following the example.

1. Это кот или собака? __**Это кот.**__

2. Это маска или знак «Стоп»? __**Это знак «Стоп».**__

3. Это нота или чек? __Это нота.__

4. Это дом или стадион? __Это дом.__

5. Это банан или лимон? __Это банан.__

6. Это банк или такси? __Это такси.__

2.6. Упражнение 8: Working on reading. The students must read words, and guess the meaning. Usually students love such exercises, because they recognize the words easily. Tell them to pay extra attention to the stress mark.

Упражнение 8   11

Read the following words, then listen to the audio and repeat after the native speaker. Consult the dictionary if you are not sure about the meaning. Write the words down.

1. лимонад __лимонад__	2. балет _____
3. анекдот _____	4. система _____
5. чемпион _____	6. металл _____
7. диплом _____	8. капитан _____
9. политика _____	10. домино _____

2.7. Introduce the new letter Ф and practice grammar: questions with the conjunction или and general questions.

Это фото.   Это фен.   – Это какао?
This is a photo.   _This is a fan._   – _Is this cocoa?_

– Это не какао. Это кофе.
– _This is not cocoa. This is coffee._

Упражнение 9

Answer the questions, following the example.

1. Это маска? __Это не маска. Это диск.__
2. Это мост? __Это не мост. Это фен.__
3. Это офис? __Это не офис. Это дом.__
4. Это банан? __Это не банан. Это лимон.__
5. Это диплом? __Это не диплом. Это фото.__
6. Это собака? __Это не собака. Это пчела.__

2. 8. Game: Sort the Words.

2. 9. The teacher is reading sentences, and the students are writing them down. Can be done at the beginning of the next lesson.

 Упражнение 10 - тест

1. Кто это? Это собака. 2. Что это? Это фото. 3. Это не банан. Это лимон. 4. Это Линда или Анна? Это Анна. 5. Это не собака. Это пчела. 6. Это не банк. Это офис. 7. Что это? Это диплом. 8. Это диск? Да, это диск. 9. Это не фен. Это пчела.

Lesson 3

Lesson Goal:

1) 4 Letters: в, г, я, р
2) Another variation of the simple question: **Что это такое?**
3) 4 Personal Pronouns: **я, он, оно, она, они**
4) Near and Distant Objects: **это, то**
5) Game: Near and Distant Objects

3.1. Introduce the letters **В, Г**.

В, Г The Russian letter **В** can be confused with the English letter **b**, but it is pronounced as **v** in **v**an.
The letter **Г** looks different from any English letter, but is pronounced as **g** in **g**ame.

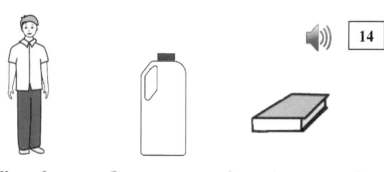

- Кто это?
- *Who is this?*
- Это человек.
- *This is a person.*

- Это молоко или вода?
- *Is this milk or water?*
- Это молоко.
- *It is milk.*

- А что это такое?
- *And what is this?*
- Это книга.
- *This is a book.*

3.2. Let's learn another variation of the simple question.

We already know simple general question: **Что это?**

But very often Russians say: Что это такое?

23

Что это такое?

Что это? = **Что это такое?** = *What is this?*

These two questions are both translated into English the same way. The word **такое** just expresses more curiosity.

 **Упражнение 11**

Ask questions about animate (living beings) and inanimate objects and answer them, following the example.

1. Что это такое? Это банан.
2. Кто это? Это человек.
3. Что это такое? Это лимон.
4. Кто это? Это пчела.
5. Что это такое? Это чашка.
6. Что это такое? Это книга.
7. Что это такое? Это молоко.
8. Кто это? Это собака.
9. Что это такое? Это фото.
10. Что это такое? Это ваза.

3.3. Introduce the letter **Я**.

Personal Pronouns: я, он, она, они

3. 4. Let's learn four personal pronouns.

я = I   он = he   она = she   они = they

Я Оля

Я Оля. Он Иван. Она Светлана. Они Антон и Нина.
I am Olya. *He is Ivan.* *She is Svetlana.* *They are Anton and Nina.*

As you see, the structure of the sentences above is very simple.

3. 5. Introducing the letter **Р**

The Letter **Р** can be challenging in the beginning. Encourage the student, if he/she has difficulties pronouncing this letter correctly. Everything comes with practice. One of the most effective ways of mastering the pronunciation is repeating after the native speaker without thinking. (Repeating after the teacher in class and working with audio at home).

Это балерина или доктор?

- Это балерина или доктор?   - Это крокодил или зебра?
  Is this a ballerina or a doctor?   *Is this a crocodile or a zebra?*

- Это балерина.   - Это зебра.
  This is a ballerina.   *It's a zebra.*

3.6. Упражнение 12: Working on reading

Упражнение 12

Read the following words, then listen to the audio and repeat after the native speaker. Consult the dictionary if you need help with translation. Write the words down.

1. метро   **метро**
2. фирма _____
3. спортсмен _____
4. актриса _____
5. Роберт _____
6. соус _____
7. Мария _____
8. паспорт _____
9. директор _____
10. класс _____
11. бизнесмен _____
12. Америка _____
13. ресторан _____
14. Калифорния _____
15. торт _____
16. Аргентина _____

Это/то

3. 7. Near and Distant Objects

There are two words in Russian that replace the phrases 'this is' and 'that is'. For near objects, we use the word **это**. For distant objects, we should use the word **то**.

это = *this is = these are*   **то** = *that is = those are*

Это яблоко.   - Что это?   Что то?-.
This is an apple.   *What is this?*   *What is that?*

То мандарин.   - Это очки.   - То стакан.
That is a tangerine. *These are glasses.*   *That is a glass.*

As you see, we use **это/то** for both singular and plural in the Present Tense.

3. 8. Упражнение 13 – Practice using **это** and **то**. It would be very useful if you could use visual aids in class such as illustration book, slides, cards, etc.

26

Упражнение 13

Create pairs of questions and answers about near and distant objects.

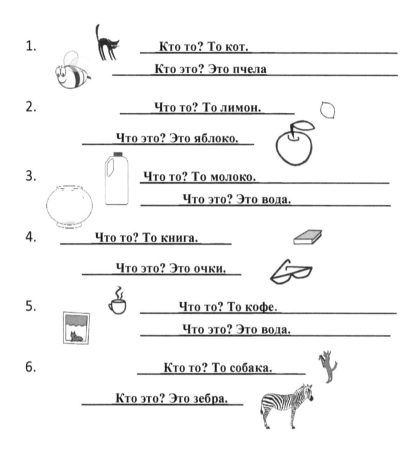

1. Кто то? То кот.
   Кто это? Это пчела
2. Что то? То лимон.
   Что это? Это яблоко.
3. Что то? То молоко.
   Что это? Это вода.
4. Что то? То книга.
   Что это? Это очки.
5. Что то? То кофе.
   Что это? Это вода.
6. Кто то? То собака.
   Кто это? Это зебра.

Упражнение 14

Answer the questions, following the example.

Образец: 1. Нет, это не доктор. Это балерина.

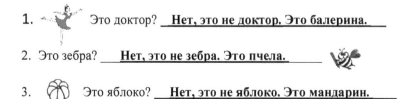

1. Это доктор? **Нет, это не доктор. Это балерина.**
2. Это зебра? **Нет, это не зебра. Это пчела.**
3. Это яблоко? **Нет, это не яблоко. Это мандарин.**

4. Это стакан? __Нет, это не стакан. Это торт.__

5. Это кофе? __Нет, это не кофе. Это сок.__

6. Это пчела? __Нет, это не пчела. Это человек.__

3. 9. Game: Near and Distant Objects

3. 10. The teacher is reading sentences – the students are writing them down. Can be done at the beginning of the next lesson.

Упражнение 15 - тест

1. Это паспорт. 2. Это спортсмен? Да, это спортсмен. 3. Это яблоко. То мандарин. 4. Кто то? То доктор. 5. Кто это? Это человек. 6. Что это? Это очки. 7. Это фирма? Да, это фирма. 8. Это не вода. Это молоко. 9. Я не Мария, я Линда. 10. Я Ольга, он Иван, она Линда, они Антон и Нина.

Lesson 4

Lesson Goal:

1) Four New Letters: ж, у, ё, й
2) Sentences with the Conjunction тоже
3) Rule: Using Conjunctions и and а
4) Names: Russian Names that End in й
5) Foreign Names
6) Game: Find the Words

4. 1. Introduce two new letters: **Ж, У**.

 Ж-ж-ж-ж....

Это муж, а это жена.   Это жук, и это тоже жук.
This is a husband and this is a wife.   *This is a beetle and this is also a beetle.*

4. 2. Introduce the conjunction **тоже** and practice using it in a sentence.

Conjunctions 'а' and 'и'

4. 3. There are two Russian conjunctions - **а** and **и** - that can be translated into English as the conjunction **and**.

Rule

Notice how the conjunctions **а** and **и** join the sentences.
When we talk about two different things, we use **а**.
When we talk about two similar things, we use **и**.

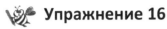
Упражнение 16

Write statements about the following pictures, using the proper conjunctions: **a** or **и**.

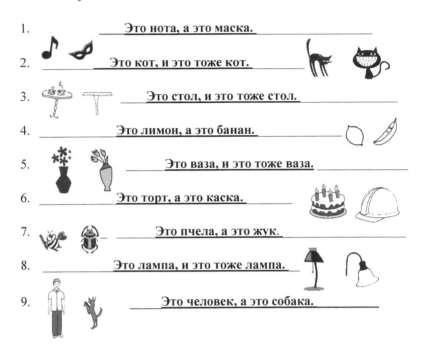

1. Это нота, а это маска.
2. Это кот, и это тоже кот.
3. Это стол, и это тоже стол.
4. Это лимон, а это банан.
5. Это ваза, и это тоже ваза.
6. Это торт, а это каска.
7. Это пчела, а это жук.
8. Это лампа, и это тоже лампа.
9. Это человек, а это собака.

4. 4. Introduce a new letter **Ё**. It is not difficult to memorize **Ё**, because this is the only letter that has two dots above it. The letter **Ё** is always stressed.

ёж — hedgehog
ёлка — fir tree
Это пилот, а то самолёт. — *This is a pilot, and this is a plane.*

4. 5. Упражнение 17

In the reading exercises pay attention to the stress. Stress matters a lot in Russian. Usually students tend to pronounce words similarly to their own tongue. For example: the word **сигнал** is pronounced in English with the stress on the first syllable. In Russian the accent falls on the second syllable. Sometimes putting the wrong stress makes the word unrecognizable.

Упражнение 17

Read the following words, then listen to the audio and repeat after the native speaker. Consult the dictionary if you need help with translation. Write the words down.

1. бокс **бокс**
2. пингвин _____
3. платформа _____
4. актёр _____
5. сувенир _____
6. пинг-понг _____
7. парк _____
8. футбол _____
9. зоопарк _____
10. гимнастика _____
11. сигнал _____
12. гараж _____
13. президент _____
14. жираф _____

4. 6. Introduce the letter **й**. Introduce the possessive pronoun for masculine objects. If the student tries to use this pronoun with a feminine or neuter object, explain that we are going to talk about genders later. At this point we will practice only one type of Possessive Pronouns – the masculine one.

 Это мой чай

Это мой брат.   Это мой стул.   Это мой чай.
This is my brother.   *This is my chair.*   *This is my tea.*

 Упражнение 18

Pretend all of the following objects are yours. Write statements about them.

1. _____ **Это мой дом.** _____

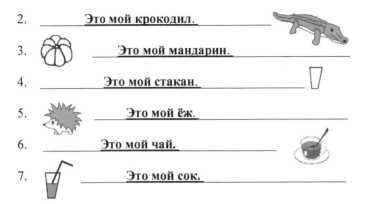

2. _____ Это мой крокодил.

3. _____ Это мой мандарин.

4. _____ Это мой стакан.

5. _____ Это мой ёж.

6. _____ Это мой чай.

7. _____ Это мой сок.

Names

 23

4. 7. Many Russian male names have **Й** at the end.

Николай, Андрей, Алексей, Григорий, Матвей.

4. 8. Foreign Names

The spelling of English names in Russian should also be practiced. There is no letter corresponding to the English letter **J**. Therefore, in Russian we must use two letters **дж** instead of **J**.

Джон   Джеймс   Джулия

Most of the time, in a foreign name the Russian letter **e** is pronounced like **э**.

Кевин (Кэвин)   Маргарет (Маргарэт)

Иногда можно встретить оба варианта, и это на произношение не влияет.

Грег = Грэг

The name **Нэнси** is more often written with **э**.

4. 9. Do упражнение 19 in writing in class. (Either turn on the audio, or read the names while the students write them down.) It will help the students to practice the writing of foreign names. If your students are slow, and you are short on time, let them write 5-10 names and the rest they will finish the rest at home.

Упражнение 19

Usually foreign names should sound similar to their language of origin. Listen to the audio, repeat after the native speaker, and try to write the following names in Russian.

1. John   **Джон**
2. Joanne **Джоан**
3. Jimmy **Джимми**
4. Julia **Джулия**
5. Bob   **Боб**
6. Nancy **Нэнси**
7. Frank **Фрэнк**
8. Deborah **Дебора**
9. Kevin **Кевин**
10. Mary **Мэри**
11. Mike **Майк**
12. Laura **Лаура**
13. Greg **Грег**
14. Jennifer **Дженнифер**
15. Joe   **Джо**
16. Patricia **Патрисия**
17. Richard **Ричард**
18. Barbara **Барбара**
19. Jason **Джейсон**
20. Margaret **Маргарет**

4. 10. Game: Find the Words

4. 11. The teacher is reading sentences – the students are writing them down. Can be done at the beginning of the next lesson

 Упражнение 20 - тест

1. Это муж, а это жена. 2. Это пчела, и это тоже пчела. 3. Кто это? Это мой брат. 4. Что это такое? Это мой сувенир. 5. То мандарин? Нет, то яблоко. 6. Это дом или офис? Это дом. 7. Это не мой чай. То мой чай. 8. Я не Дженифер. Я Патрисия. 9. Что то такое? То чай. 10. Это стол? Нет, это не стол. 11. Что это? Это стул.

Lesson 5

Lesson Goal:

1) Four New Letters: **х, ц, ь, ъ**
2) The Role of the Soft and Hard Signs in the Word
3) Gender of the Nouns
4) **Where: Где стол? Вот он.**
5) Game: **Sort the Nouns**

5.1. Introduce two new letters: **Х, Ц**. 25

The letter **X** is another tricky one. It looks like English X but is pronounced similarly to the **h** in **h**at.

The letter **Ц** looks different from any English letter but is pronounced exactly like the **ts** in boots. It often takes time to learn to pronounce this letter correctly.

| хлеб | ухо | Хо́лодно! | пи́цца |
| *bread* | *ear* | *It's cold!* | *pizza* |

 Упражнение 21   26

Read the following words, then listen to the audio and repeat after the native speaker. Consult the dictionary if you need help with translation. Write the words down.

1. киоск **киоск**   2. хоккей _____

3. аэропорт _____   4. лимузин _____

5. бадминтон _____ 6. информация _____

7. регби _____ 8. кобра _____

9. космос _____ 10. музей _____

11. полиция _____ 12. суп _____

Упражнение 22

Answer the questions, following the example.

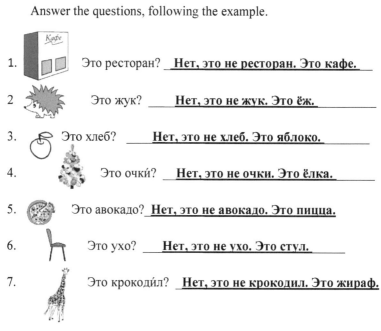

1. Это ресторан? **Нет, это не ресторан. Это кафе.**
2. Это жук? **Нет, это не жук. Это ёж.**
3. Это хлеб? **Нет, это не хлеб. Это яблоко.**
4. Это очки? **Нет, это не очки. Это ёлка.**
5. Это авокадо? **Нет, это не авокадо. Это пицца.**
6. Это ухо? **Нет, это не ухо. Это стул.**
7. Это крокоди́л? **Нет, это не крокодил. Это жираф.**

Ь, Ъ

5. 2. Introduce two new letters: **ь, ъ**. These two letters are silent.

Это семья.

Это жильё.

This is a family.   *This is place to live.*

ь – the soft sign has two main functions:

1) it works as a separation sign when it is followed by a vowel:

семья   жильё

2) it softens the preceding consonant:

мать = *mother*   контроль = *control*   конь = *horse*

In order to feel the difference the soft sign makes, listen to the audio and repeat after the native speaker.

| семья – семя | жильё – жилё | братья - братя |

| конь – кон | контроль – контрол | фильм - филм |

ъ – the hard sign works as a separation sign in the same way as the soft sign does. In ancient times **ъ** was used a lot, but now it is used very rarely. In modern Russian there are few words with the hard sign.

| въезд | объём | подъём |

въезд = *entrance* (for cars)   объём = *volume*   подъём = *ascent*

5. 3. Gender of the nouns

Gender of the Nouns

All Russian nouns can be divided into three groups, according to their gender: masculine, feminine, and neuter. In the majority of cases, you can tell the gender of the word by its ending.

Nouns that end in the soft sign can be either masculine or feminine. In this case, you can learn the gender from the dictionary.

Он, она, оно

 - он: сто**л**, музе**й**, кон**ь** – masculine nouns end in a consonant or in a soft sign;

 - она: Англи**я**, ёлк**а**, мат**ь** – feminine nouns end in **a** or **я** or in a soft sign;

 - оно: каф**é**, ябло**ко** - neuter nouns end in **o** or **e**.

And of course there are exceptions:
папа is a masculine word.

5. 4. Where: Questions and Answers

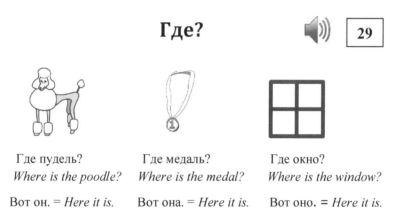

Где пудель?　　　　Где медаль?　　　　Где окно?
Where is the poodle?　*Where is the medal?*　*Where is the window?*

Вот он. = *Here it is.*　Вот она. = *Here it is.*　Вот оно. = *Here it is.*

The pronouns **он** and **она** are used for both **living beings** and **inanimate objects**. The pronoun **оно** is used **only for inanimate objects**.

5. 5. Practice determining the noun's gender.

 **Упражнение 23**

Divide the following words into three columns according to gender.

Ма́ма, па́па, челове́к, ва́за, ко́фе, кни́га, мета́лл, окно́, пчела́, у́хо, соба́ка, чемпио́н, Григо́рий, я́блоко, семья́, балери́на, кафе́, такси́, контро́ль, меда́ль, метро́, музе́й, авока́до, те́ннис, фо́то, зе́бра, меню́.

он	она	оно
папа	мама	окно
человек	ваза	ухо
кофе	книга	яблоко
металл	пчела	кафе
чемпион	собака	такси
Григорий	семья	метро
контроль	балерина	авокадо
музей	медаль	фото
теннис	зебра	меню

Упражнение 24

Write pairs of questions and answers about the following pictures, as in the example.

1. Где крокодил? Вот он.
2. Где мандарин? Вот он.
3. Где кофе? Вот он.
4. Где хлеб? Вот он.
5. Где пицца? Вот она.
6. Где такси? Вот оно.
7. Где стул? Вот он.
8. Где чай? Вот он.
9. Где кафе? Вот оно.
10. Где ёж? Вот он.
11. Где ёлка? Вот она.

12. _____ Где яблоко? Вот оно. _____

13. _____ Где жираф? Вот он. _____

14. _____ Где зебра? Вот она. _____

5. 6. Game: Sort the Nouns

5. 7. The teacher is reading sentences – the students are writing them down. Can be done at the beginning of the next lesson.

Упражнение 25 - тест

1. Холодно? Да, холодно. 2. Это хлеб или пицца? Это хлеб. 3. Это не офис. Это музей. 4. Это суп, а то салат. 5. Он директор? Да, он директор. 6. Где менеджер? Вот он. 7. Где такси? Вот оно. 8. Где медаль? Вот она. 9. Я Джулия, он Джон, они Ганс и Моника. 10. Он Николай, и он тоже Николай. 11. Где въезд? Вот он.

Lesson 6

Lesson Goal:

1) Four New Letters: **ш, щ, ы, ю**
2) Difference in Pronunciation between **ы** and **и**
3) Three New Personal Pronouns: **ты, вы, мы**
4) Counting: **0 – 10**
5) Game: **Guess the Word**

6. 1. Introduce two new letters: **Ш, Щ**.

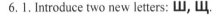

Это ба́бушка. Это де́душка. Это шокола́д.
This is grandma. *This is grandpa.* *This is chocolate.*

борщ = *beetroot soup*   вещь = *a thing*   щено́к = a puppy

The letter **ш** is always hard and is pretty easy to pronounce. The letter **щ** looks similar to **ш**, but has a little 'leg', and is pronounced softer: as the **shsh** in Engli**sh sh**ip. Ask the students to repeat pairs if syllables with **ш** and **щ**:

      ша – ща   шу- щу   шё – щё   ше- ще

Упражнение 26

Read the following words, then listen to the audio and repeat after the native speaker. Consult the dictionary if you need help with translation. Write the words down.

1. Чика́го **Чикаго**
2. Вашингто́н _____
3. центр _____
4. шокола́д _____
5. тра́нспорт _____
6. Шéрон _____
7. шик _____
8. секрета́рша _____
9. диало́г _____
10. теа́тр _____
11. Ната́ша _____
12. шок _____

Упражнение 27

Create short dialogues, following the example.

Образец: 1. Это ёлка?
Нет, это не ёлка.
Кто это?
Это жираф.

1. Это ёлка? _____
2. Это шоколад? **Нет, это не шоколад. Что это? Это медаль.**
3. Это щенок? **Нет, это не щенок. Кто это? Это ёж.**
4. Это пудель? **Нет, это не пудель. Что это? Это пицца.**
5. Это вещь? **Нет, это не вещь. Кто это? Это балерина**
6. Это борщ? **Нет, это не борщ. Это книга.**
7. Это музей? **Нет, это не музей. Это хлеб.**

6. 2. Introduce the letter **Ы**. The letter **Ы** is pronounced similarly to the **i** in sit. The letter **Ы** is often confused with **И**. Listen to the pairs of syllables with different consonants and compare the sounds.

Don't worry if the student does not feel the difference between these two letters. Everything comes with practice. Often students understand the difference when they repeat words, rather than syllables. (Audio Track 33)

Ы-И

| мы – ми | вы – ви | ры – ри | ны – ни | ты – ти |
| сы – си | пы – пи | бы – би | кы – ки | ды – ди |

Personal Pronouns

6. 3. In Lesson 3 we learned four Personal Pronouns: **я, он, она, они**. In this lesson we will learn three more: **ты, вы, мы**.

ты = you (informal)   вы = *you (polite)*   мы = *we*

There are two forms of addressing people in Russian: formal (or polite) - **вы** and informal - **ты**. The general rule is:

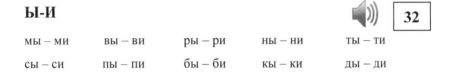

You → вы → for adults, until asked to do otherwise
    → ты → for children

Я Оля. | Ты Иван. | Вы Светлана. | Мы Нина и Антон.
I am Ivan. | *You are Olya.* | *You are Svetlana.* | *We are Anton and Nina.*

6. 4. As was mentioned earlier, the letter **ы** needs to be practiced more. Let's practice this letter in the words.

   34

ры́ба = *fish*   цветы́ = *flowers*   сыр = *cheese*

6. 5. Introduce the letter **Ю**.

 35

Нью Йо́рк   Ю́лия   Ю́рий

Do Exercise 28 orally in class and then ask the students to do it in writing as homework.

Упражнение 28   36

Read the following words, then listen to the audio and repeat after the native speaker. Consult the dictionary if you need help with translation. Write the words down.

1. Нью-Дже́рси **Нью-Джерси**   2. гиппопотам _____

3. журна́л _____   4. мини́стр _____

5. му́зыка _____   6. джи́нсы _____

7. визи́т _____   8. спорт _____

9. мира́ж _____   10. инструме́нт _____

11. саксофо́н _____   12. инструмент _____

13. туале́т _____   14. клуб _____

Упражнение 29

Answer the following questions, as in the example.

1.   Это пчела́? **Нет, это не пчела. Это пудель**

2. Это цветы? **Нет, это не цветы. Это рыба.**

3. Это хлеб? **Нет, это не хлеб. Это сыр.**

4. Это бабушка? **Нет, это не бабушка. Это дедушка.**

5. Это ёлка? **Нет, это не ёлка. Это щенок.**

6. Это стул? **Нет, это не стул. Это окно.**

7. Это борщ? **Нет, это не борщ. Это цветы.**

6. 6. Counting: 0 – 10

Посчитаем! 0-10   37

0 – ноль	1 – оди́н	2 – два	3 – три
4 – четы́ре	5 – пять	6 – шесть	7 – семь
8 – во́семь	9 – де́вять	10 – де́сять	

6. 7. Game: Guess the Word

6. 7. The teacher is reading sentences – the students are writing them down. Can be done at the beginning of the next lesson.

Упражнение 30 - тест

1. Где бабушка? Вот она. 2. Где сыр? Вот он. 3. Где щенок? Вот он. 4. Это борщ или суп? Это борщ. 5. Это мой брат. 6. Мы Саша и Даша. 7. Кто это? Это мой дедушка. 8. Кто то? То мой папа. 9. Это офис, и то тоже офис. 10. Ты кто? Я Оля. 11. Вы Никита.

Test 1

Final Exam has two parts:

Part 1 – Listening Comprehension and Spelling:

The first two tasks (Задание 1, 2): The teacher reads the phrases and the students choose the correct answers in their handouts. (The teacher may repeat the sentences if needed.)

Part 2 – Grammar and Vocabulary. Students do this part on their own by choosing the correct answers in their handouts.

The teacher prints out the handouts before the test. For Student's handouts please, contact us at info@russianstepbystep.com

Part 1 – Listening Comprehension and Spelling

❖ **Задание 1**. Listen to the phrases the teacher reads to you and choose the correct answer.

1. Это молоко. _____

    а. Это малако.

    б. Эта малако.

    в. Это молоко.

2. То очки. _____

    а. Это ачки.

    б. То очки.

    в. Это очки.

3. Это жук, и то тоже жук. _____

    а. Это жук, и то тоже жук.

    б. То жук, то тоже жук.

    в. Эта жук, и то тоже жук.

Ответы к заданию 1:
1 – в; 2 – б; 3 – а;

❖ **Задание 2.** Listen to the phrases the teacher reads to you and choose the correct answer.

4. Это мой брат Юрий. _____

   а. Это мой брат Юри.

   б. Эта мой брат Юрий.

   в. Это мой брат Юрий.

5. То Нью-Йорк _____

   а. То Ню Ёорк.

   б. То Нью-Йорк.

   в. То Нью Ёорк.

6. Это не собака, а щенок. _____

   а. Эта не собака, а щенок.

   б. Это не собака, а шенок.

   в. Это не собака, а щенок.

7. Это вещь, и то тоже вещь. _____

   а. Это вещь, и то тоже вещь.

   б. Эта вешь, и то тоже вешь.

   в. Это вещ, и то тоже вещ.

Ответы к заданию 2:

4 – в;   5 – б;   6 – в;   7 – а;

Part 2 - Grammar and Vocabulary

❖ **Задание 3.** Read the following questions and choose the correct answer. (Gender agreement)

8. Где пудель? _____

   а. Вот он.

   б. Вот она.

   в. Вот оно.

9. Где чашка? _____

   а. Вот он.

   б. Вот она.

   в. Вот оно.

10. Где меню? _____

    а. Вот он.

    б. Вот она.

    в. Вот оно.

Ответы к заданию 3:

8 – а;   9– б;   10 – в;

❖ **Задание 4.** Choose the correct phrase with the corresponding Personal Pronoun. (Personal Pronouns)

11. Маша _____

    а. Ты Маша.

    б. Вы Маша.

    в. Мы Маша.

12. доктор _____

    а. Ты доктор.

    б. Вы доктор.

    в. Мы доктор.

    г. Они доктор

13. Рита и Саша _____

    а. Ты Рита и Саша.

    б. Мы Рита и Саша.

    в. Она Рита и Саша.

Ответы к заданию 4:

11 – а; 12 – б; 13 – б;

❖   **Задание 5.** Choose the correct word for the corresponding number. (Numbers)

14. 5 _____

    а. пять

    б. шесть

    в. четыре

15. 9 _____

    а. десять

    б. семь

    в. девять

16. 7 _____

    а. восемь

    б. семь

    в. девять

Ответы к заданию 5:

14 – а;   15 – в;   16 – б;

❖   **Задание 6.** Choose the correct word for the corresponding picture. (Vocabulary)

17. каска _____

    а. маска

    б. каска

    в. цветы

18. рыба _____

    а. собака

    б. рыба

    в. жук

19. пчела _____

    а. пчела

    б. рыба

    в. жук

20. сыр

    а. хлеб

    б. самолёт

    в. сыр

21. ёж

    а. стакан

    б. ёж

    в. очки

22. книга

    а. чай

    б. яблоко

    в. книга

23. ёлка

    а. ёлка

    б. мост

    в. человек

24. самолёт

    а. самолёт

б. пилот

в. вода

25. стул

   а. стол

   б. стул

   в. ёлка

26. хлеб

   а. пицца

   б. яблоко

   в. хлеб

27. **ухо**

   а. жильё

   б. ухо

   в. холодно

Ответы к заданию 6:

17 – б;   18 – б;   19 – а;   20 – в;   21 – б;   22 – в;   23 – а;

24 – а;   25 – б;   26 – в;   27. б.

Grammar Tables

Personal Pronouns

I	You Informal	You Polite	We	He	She	It Neuter object	They
я	ты	вы	мы	он	она	оно	они

Numbers

0	1	2	3
ноль	один	два	три
4	5	6	7
четрые	пять	шесть	семь
8	9	10	
восемь	девять	десять	

Dictionaries

Russian-English Dictionary

Abbreviations

adj – adjective
adv – adverb
f – feminine
m – masculine
n – neuter

pl – plural
refl – reflexive verb
sing – singular
sfa – short form adjective

If a word is pronounced in a different way from the rule, it has the transcription in brackets.

For example: in the word здра́вствуйте [здра́ствуйте] the first letter **в** is not pronounced.

А

а and, but, oh, so
абрико́с apricot
авока́до avocado
авто́бус bus
администра́ция administration
а́дрес address
аква́риум aquarium
актёр actor
актри́са actress
алфави́т alphabet
Аме́рика America
анекдо́т anecdote, funny story
А́фрика Africa
аэропо́рт airport

Б

ба́бушка grandmother
бага́ж baggage
бадминто́н badminton
бале́т ballet
балери́на ballerina
балко́н balcony
бана́н banana
банк bank
баскетбо́л basketball
бассе́йн swimming pool
бегемо́т hippopotamus
бизнесме́н businessman
блок block
бокс boxing
борщ beet (beetroot) soup
босс boss
брасле́т bracelet
брат brother
бриз sea breeze
бу́ква lettter
бума́га paper

В

ва́за vase
вещь thing
вода́ water
въезд entrance (for vehicles)
вы you (polite *sing/pl*)

Г

гара́ж garage
где where
геогра́фия geography
гео́лог geologist
геро́й hero
гимна́стика gymnastics
гость *m* guest
гру́ппа group

Д

да yes
де́вочка little girl
де́вять nine
де́душка grandfather
десе́рт dessert
де́сять ten
джи́нсы jeans
диало́г dialogue
диза́йнер designer
дипло́м diploma
дире́ктор director
диск disk
до́ктор doctor
докуме́нт document
до́ллар dollar
дом house, building

дочь daughter

Е

ещё still, yet, more

Ё

ёж hedgehog
ёлка fir tree

Ж

жена́ wife
жильё housing, accomodation
жира́ф giraffe
жук beetle
журна́л *n* magazine

З

здра́вствуйте [здраствуйте] Hello
зе́бра zebra
знак sign
зо́на zone
зоопа́рк zoo

И

и and
и́ли or
И́ндия India
инжене́р engineer
информа́ция information
Испа́ния Spain

Ита́лия Italy

К

кака́о cocoa
Калифо́рния California
калькуля́тор calculator
Кана́да Canada
кана́л channel
капита́н captain
кафе́ café
ке́мпинг campsite
кио́ск kiosk
класс classroom, grade
клие́нт client
клуб club
кни́га book
ко́бра cobra
колле́га colleague
ко́лледж college
компа́ния company
компози́тор composer
компью́тер computer
кондиционе́р air conditioner
контро́ль *m* control
конце́рт concert
конь *m* horse
коридо́р bullfight, corridor
ко́смос cosmos, (outer) space
костю́м suit, costume
кот cat
ко́фе *m* coffee
крокоди́л crocodile
кто who

Л

ла́мпа lamp
ли́лия lily
лимо́н lemon
лимона́д lemonade
лимузи́н limo
литерату́ра literature
литр liter

М

майоне́з mayonnaise
ма́льчик little boy
ма́ма mom
мандари́н tangerine
ма́ска mask
масса́ж massage
матема́тика math
мать mother
ма́фия mafia
маши́на car, machine
меда́ль *f* medal
медсестра́ nurse (female)
Ме́ксика Mexico
ме́неджер manager
меню́ menu
мета́лл metal
метро́ metro
микроско́п microscope
мини́стр minister
ми́нус minus
мину́та minute
мира́ж mirage
мой my
молоко́ milk
моме́нт moment
мо́ре sea

муж   husband
музе́й   museum
му́зыка   music
мы   we

Н

не   not
нет   no
ноль   *m*   zero
но́мер   number
нос   nose
но́та   note
Нью Дже́рси   New Jersey
Нью Йорк   New York
нюа́нс   nuance

О

образе́ц   example
объём   volume
огуре́ц   cucumber
оди́н   one
о́зеро   lake
окно́   window
он   he
она́   she
оно́   it, a neuter object
они́   they
о́пера   opera
орке́стр   orchestra
отли́чно   *adv*   perfect, excellent
о́фис   office
о́чень   *adv*   very
очки́   glasses, spectacles

П

панора́ма   panorama
па́па   dad
парк   park
парла́мент   parliament
пассажи́р   passenger
па́спорт   passport
пацие́нт   [пациэнт]   patient
пило́т   pilot
пи́цца   pizza
план   plan
платфо́рма   platform
плюс   plus
пожа́луйста   [пажалуста]   welcome, please
пока́   bye
поли́тика   politics
помидо́р   tomato
поня́тно!   *adv*   I see! It's clear!
посчита́ем   [пащитаем]   let's count; let's calculate
президе́нт   president
приве́т   Hi! (informal)
при́нтер   printer
прия́тно   *adv*   pleasant
пробле́ма   problem
программи́ст   programmer
прое́кт   project
прости́те   I am sorry
профе́ссия   profession
профе́ссор   professor
пу́дель   *m*   poodle
пчела́   bee
пять   five

Р

ра́дио radio
рестора́н restaurant
реце́пт recipe
ро́бот robot
ро́за rose
Росси́я Russia
рубль *m* ruble
ру́сский *adj* Russian
ру́чка pen
ры́ба fish

С

саксофо́н saxophone
сала́т salad
сантиме́тр centimeter
сви́тер sweater
секрета́рша secretary (female)
семья́ family
се́рый gray
сигна́л signal
ско́лько how much, how many
слова́рь *m* dictionary
слон elephant
снег snow
соба́ка dog
сок juice
со́лнце sun
со́ус sauce
спаси́бо thank you
спорт sport
спортсме́н sportsman, athlete
стадио́н stadium
стака́н glass
станда́рт standard

стол table
стоп *n* stop
студе́нт student
стул chair
сувени́р souvenir
суп soup
сыр cheese

Т

теа́тр theater
текст text
телеви́зор TV set
телефо́н phone
те́ннис tennis
тепе́рь *adv* now, nowadays
то́же also
торт cake
трамва́й tram
тра́нспорт transport
три three
тролле́йбус trolleybus
трюк trick
туале́т toilet, restroom
тури́ст tourist
ты you (informal singular)

У

упражне́ние exercise
уро́к lesson

Ф

факс fax
фе́рмер farmer (male)
фи́зика physics

фильм film
фирма firm
фо́то photo
фотогра́фия photograph
фра́за phrase
Фра́нция France
фрукт fruit
футбо́л soccer

Х

хлеб bread
хокке́й hockey
хо́лодно *adv* cold
хорошо́ *adv* good, OK, well

Ц

цветы́ flowers
центр center

Ч

чай *n* tea
часы́ *pl* clock, watch
ча́шка cup
чек *n* check
челове́к person
чемпио́н champion

четы́ре four
что [што] what, that

Ш

шесть six
шко́ла school
шокола́д chocolate
шо́рты shorts

Щ

щено́к puppy

Э

эконо́мика economy
э́то this

Ю

юри́ст lawyer

Я

я I
я́блоко *n* apple

English-Russian Dictionary

A

accommodation жильё
actor актёр
address *n* а́дрес
administration администра́ция
Africa А́фрика
airport аэропо́рт
alphabet алфави́т
also то́же
America Аме́рика
and а, и
anecdote анекдо́т
animal зверь
apple *n* я́блоко
apricot абрико́с
aquarium аква́риум
athlete спортсме́н
avocado авока́до

B

badminton бадминто́н
baggage бага́ж
balcony балко́н
ballerina балери́на
ballet балет
banana бана́н
bank банк
basketball баскетбо́л
bee пчела́
beetle жук
beet (beetroot) soup борщ

block блок
book кни́га
boss босс
boxing бокс
boy ма́льчик (little)
bracelet брасле́т
brother брат
bus авто́бус
businessman бизнесме́н
bye пока́ (informal)

C

café кафе́
cake торт
calculator калькуля́тор
California Калифо́рния
camera фотоаппара́т
campsite ке́мпинг
Canada Кана́да
captain капита́н
car маши́на
cat кот
center *n* центр
chair стул
champion чемпио́н
channel кана́л
check *n* чек
cheese сыр
chemistry хи́мия
chocolate *n* шокола́д
classroom класс

classroom класс
client клие́нт
clock *pl* часы́
club клуб
cobra ко́бра
cocoa кака́о
code код
coffee *m* ко́фе
cold *adv* хо́лодно
colleague колле́га
college ко́лледж
company компа́ния
computer компью́тер
comrade това́рищ
concert конце́рт
conditioner кондиционе́р
control *m* контро́ль
corridor коридо́р
cosmos ко́смос
costume костю́м, наря́д
crocodile крокоди́л
cucumber огуре́ц
cup ча́шка

D

dad па́па
daughter дочь
day *m* день
designer дизайне́р
dialogue диало́г
dictionary *m* слова́рь
diploma дипло́м
director дире́ктор
discotheque дискоте́ка
disk диск
doctor врач

document докуме́нт
dog соба́ка
dollar до́ллар

E

economy эконо́мика
eight во́семь
elephant слон
engineer инжене́р
entrance (for vehicles) въезд
example образе́ц
excellent *adv* отли́чно
excuse me извини́те
exercise упражне́ние

F

family семья́
farmer фе́рмер
fax факс
film фильм
firm фи́рма
fir tree ёлка
fish ры́ба
five пять
flowers цветы́
four четы́ре
France Фра́нция
fruit фрукт

G

garage гара́ж
gallery галере́я
giraffe жира́ф
girl де́вочка

glass стака́н
glasses очки́ (spectacles)
good *adv* хорошо́
grade класс
grandfather де́душка
grandmother ба́бушка
group гру́ппа
guest *m* гость

H

he он
hedgehog ёж
Hello! Здра́вствуйте! [здраствуйте]
hero геро́й
hippopotamus бегемо́т
home *n* дом
horse *m* конь
house дом
housing жильё
how как
how much, how many ско́лько
human being челове́к
husband муж

I

I я
if е́сли
India И́ндия
information информа́ция
Internet интерне́т
it (neuter object) оно́
Italy Ита́лия

J

jeans джи́нсы
juice сок

K

kiosk кио́ск

L

lamp ла́мпа, торше́р (floor lamp)
language язы́к
limo лимузи́н
lemon лимо́н
lemonade лимона́д
lesson уро́к
letter бу́ква
lily ли́лия
liter литр
literature литерату́ра

M

mafia ма́фия
magazine журна́л
manager ме́неджер
mask ма́ска
massage масса́ж
math матема́тика
medal *f* меда́ль
menu меню́
metal мета́лл
metro метро́
Mexico Ме́ксика
microscope микроско́п

milk молоко́
minister мини́стр
minus ми́нус
minute мину́та
mirage мира́ж
mistake оши́бка
mobile моби́льный
mom ма́ма
moment моме́нт
Moscow Москва́
mother мать
motorcycle мотоци́кл
museum музе́й
music му́зыка
my мой

N

New Jersey Нью Дже́рси
New York Нью Йорк
next to ря́дом с
night *f* ночь
nine де́вять
no нет
not не
note но́та
now сейча́с [сичас], тепе́рь
nuance нюа́нс
number но́мер
nurse медсестра́ (female)
    медбра́т (male)

O

object вещь
office кабине́т, о́фис
Oh! А!

OK *adv* ла́дно, хорошо́
one оди́н
opera о́пера
or и́ли
orange *n* апельси́н
orchestra орке́стр

P

panorama панора́ма
paper бума́га
park парк
Parliament парла́мент
passenger пассажи́р
passport па́спорт
patient пацие́нт [пациэнт]
pen ру́чка
perfect *adv* отли́чно
person челове́к
pharmacy апте́ка
phone телефо́н
photo фо́то
photograph фотогра́фия
phrase фра́за
pilot *n* пило́т
pizza пи́цца
plan план
platform платфо́рма
pleasant *adv* прия́тно
please пожа́луйста
    [пажалуста]
plus плюс
politics *sing* поли́тика
poodle *m* пу́дель
president президе́нт
printer при́нтер
problem пробле́ма, вопро́с

profession профе́ссия
professor профе́ссор
programmer программи́ст
project прое́кт
puppy щено́к
puree пюре́

Q

question *n* вопро́с

R

radio ра́дио
rain *m* дождь
restaurant рестора́н
restroom туале́т
robot ро́бот
rose *n* ро́за
ruble *m* рубль
rugby ре́гби
Russia Росси́я
Russian *adj* ру́сский

S

salad сала́т
sauce со́ус
saxophone саксофо́н
school шко́ла
sea мо́ре
sea breeze бриз
secretary секрета́рь (male),
    секрета́рша (female)
seven семь
she она́
shorts шо́рты

sign (symbol) *n* знак
sign *v* подпи́сывать
signal сигна́л
sister сестра́
six шесть
snow *n* снег
so а
soccer футбо́л
son сын
soup суп
souvenir сувени́р
Spain Испа́ния
sport спорт
stadium стадио́н
standard станда́рт
stop *n* остано́вка, стоп
student студе́нт
subtitle субти́тр
suit *n* костю́м
sweater сви́тер
system систе́ма

T

table стол
tangerine мандари́н
ten де́сять
tennis те́ннис
text текст
thank you спаси́бо
theater теа́тр
they они́
thing вещь
this э́то
three три
toilet туале́т
tomato помидо́р
tongue язы́к

tourist тури́ст
tram трамва́й
transport тра́нспорт
trick трюк
trolleybus тролле́йбус
TV set телеви́зор
two два

U

university университе́т

V

vase ва́за
very о́чень
volume объём

W

watch *pl* часы́
water вода́
we мы
welcome пожа́луйста
  [пажалуста]
well хорошо́
watch *n pl* часы́
where где
wife жена́
who кто
window окно́

Y

yes да
you (polite singular/*pl*) вы

Z

zebra зе́бра
zero *m* ноль
zip code и́ндекс
zone зо́на
zoo зоопа́рк

Available Titles

Adult Learner's Series:

1. **Student Book 1 Beginner:** Russian Step By Step: School Edition (Book & Audio)
2. **Teacher's Manual 1 Beginner:** Russian Step By Step: School Edition
3. **Student Book 2 Low Intermediate:** Russian Step By Step: School Edition (Book & Audio)
4. **Teacher's Manual 2 Low Intermediate**: Russian Step By Step: School Edition
5. **Student Book Intermediate 3:** Russian Step By Step: School Edition (Book & Audio)
6. **Teacher's Manual 3 Intermediate**: Russian Step By Step: School Edition
7. **Student Book 4 Upper Intermediate:** Russian Step By Step: School Edition (Book & Audio)
8. **Teacher's Manual 4 Upper Intermediate**: Russian Step By Step: School Edition
9. Russian Handwriting 1: **Propisi 1**
10. Russian Handwriting 2: **Propisi 2**
11. Russian Handwriting 3: **Propisi 3**
12. **Verbs of Motion**: Workbook 1
13. **Verbs of Motion**: Workbook 2

Children's Series: Age 3 - 7

1. Azbuka 1: **Coloring Russian Alphabet:** Азбука-раскраска (Step 1)
2. Azbuka 2: **Playing with Russian Letters:** Занимательная азбука (Step2)
3. Azbuka 3: **Beginning with Syllables:** Мои первые слоги (Step 3)
4. Azbuka 4: **Continuing with Syllables**: Продолжаем изучать слоги (Step 4)
5. **Animal Names and Sounds**: Кто как говорит Part 1
6. **Animal Names and Sounds: Coloring Book:** Кто как говорит Part 2
7. Propisi for Preschoolers 1: **Russian Letters: Trace and Learn:** Тренируем пальчики (Step 1)

Children's Series: Age 8 - 14

1. **Workbook 1:** Reading Russian Step By Step for Children (Book & Audio)
2. **Teacher's Manual 1**: Russian Step By Step for Children
3. **Student Book 2:** Russian Step By Step for Children (Book & Audio)
4. **Teacher's Manual 2:** Russian Step By Step for Children
5. **Workbook 3:** Reading Russian Step By Step for Children (Book & Audio)
6. **Teacher's Manual 3**: Russian Step By Step for Children
7. **Workbook 4:** Reading Russian Step By Step for Children (Book & Audio)
8. **Teacher's Manual 4**: Russian Step By Step for Children
9. Russian Handwriting 1: **Propisi 1**
10. Russian Handwriting 2: **Propisi 2**
11. Russian Handwriting 3: **Propisi 3**

Made in United States
Troutdale, OR
09/13/2023

12890656R00046